SUZANNE STABILE

WITH *Laura Addis*

The

JOURNEY TOWARD WHOLENESS

Study Guide

An imprint of InterVarsity Press
Downers Grove, Illinois

InterVarsity Press
P.O. Box 1400, Downers Grove, IL 60515-1426
ivpress.com
email@ivpress.com

InterVarsity Press® is the book-publishing division of InterVarsity Christian Fellowship/USA®, a movement
of students and faculty active on campus at hundreds of universities, colleges, and schools of nursing in the
United States of America, and a member movement of the International Fellowship of Evangelical Students.
For information about local and regional activities, visit intervarsity.org.

While any stories in this book are true, some names and identifying information may have been changed to
protect the privacy of individuals.

The publisher cannot verify the accuracy or functionality of website URLs used in this book beyond the date of
publication.

Cover design and image composite: David Fassett
Interior design: Daniel van Loon
Images: white moving clouds: © Matt Anderson Photography / Moment / Getty Images
    branch of green leaves: © Pramote Polyamate / Moment / Getty Images
    technology human head: © VICTOR HABBICK VISIONS / Getty Images

ISBN 978-1-5140-0214-8 (print)
ISBN 978-1-5140-0215-5 (digital)

Printed in the United States of America ∞

InterVarsity Press is committed to ecological stewardship and to the conservation of natural resources in all our
operations. This book was printed using sustainably sourced paper.

Library of Congress Cataloging-in-Publication Data

Names: Stabile, Suzanne, author.

Title: The journey toward wholeness study guide / Suzanne Stabile ; with Laura Addis.

Description: Downers Grove, IL : InterVarsity Press, [2021]

Identifiers: LCCN 2021030767 (print) | LCCN 2021030768 (ebook) | ISBN 9781514002148 (print) |
    ISBN 9781514002155 (digital)

Subjects: LCSH: Self-actualization (Psychology)—Religious aspects—Christianity—Textbooks. |
    Enneagram—Textbooks. | Spiritual formation—Textbooks.

Classification: LCC BV4598.2 .S72252 2021 (print) | LCC BV4598.2 (ebook) | DDC 158.1/5—dc23

LC record available at https://lccn.loc.gov/2021030767

LC ebook record available at https://lccn.loc.gov/2021030768

P	21	20	19	18	17	16	15	14	13	12	11	10	9	8	7	6	5	4	3	2	1
Y	39	38	37	36	35	34	33	32	31	30	29	28	27	26	25	24	23	22	21

CONTENTS

INTRODUCTION

Welcome! However you came to be reading this study guide, I'm so very glad you're here. I wrote *The Journey Toward Wholeness* because I believe we all have the ability to grow, change, and experience transformation—spiritually, emotionally, and psychologically. Growth in all of these ways takes time, and it can even be painful, but it offers us a gift: the gift that we don't have to do things the way we've always done them.

I'm convinced that you can't change what you can't name. Without accountability, our habitual and predictable behavior— the average space of our Enneagram type—wins out most of the time. Without intentional plans for growing and changing, we are often unprepared for the challenges that we are sure to face, and the result is that we fall back into average space in our number and make our way in the world just the same way we always have. As a result, we are faced with the same challenges over and over because we keep operating in the same way we always have.

The Enneagram teaches us that there are nine ways of being in the world and it highlights the nine habitual, predictable ways that we get ourselves into trouble. Without hearing the stories of how challenging it has been for other people, we end up thinking we are the only one struggling. The struggle isn't the same for each of us, but it can be shared. We can always learn from the other eight ways of seeing the world, and learning always has the potential to lead to growth.

I have always had a general desire to do better and be better. But until I learned the Enneagram, I didn't have an identified understanding of the areas in my life that needed my attention. The first time I heard it taught I was able to name, almost immediately, the places in my life that were working and the situations where I had to make necessary changes. Hearing about my number literally changed everything for me in terms of how I saw myself and how I saw other people. That is the primary reason why I decided to dedicate the remainder of my career to teaching the Enneagram: because it offers specific, tangible ways to move toward balance and wholeness.

My experience is that almost all of the teaching about spiritual formation includes information about balance and integration, but it's rare to find a method or a book or a teacher offering instruction about *how* to balance or integrate.

The Journey Toward Wholeness is designed to support growth and stability in a time of enormous transition. We aren't the first to face this challenge of transformation in a time of liminality and we won't be the last. It's uncomfortable and unpredictable and uncertain, but it can also be a time for new understanding about ourselves, our culture, and our capacity for accommodating change. The truth is, we all have experienced shorter amounts of time in liminal space. Upon hearing the definition of *liminality*, I suspect most seniors in high school would say that's where they find themselves. College graduates find that the time between graduation, getting a job, finding a place to live, and starting their "new life" perfectly defines liminality. The last month of pregnancy, buying and then moving into a new home, completing the plans to move to a new job in a new state, preparing for retirement, embracing limitations that slowly approach—all liminal space. Some have said that liminal space is the most teachable space, and I agree, but we have to be open to learning from it. That will be part of your work as you engage in this study.

You will gain much insight about why you do the very things you don't want to do, and I hope you allow yourself to dream about who you can be as a result of what you learn. And my dream for you is that you come away from this experience with more hope and more peace than you would have imagined. The truth is we can all be better friends, better coworkers, better family members, and better advocates for ourselves and our ways of seeing the world. The combination of liminal space and Enneagram wisdom offers an opportunity for all of us to move beyond wishing we could be different or healthier or better. We can be.

WHAT TO EXPECT IN EACH SESSION

The sessions are designed for sixty to ninety minutes of discussion each week. Each includes the following components.

- **Check In:** a time for your group to reconnect and share observations based on the previous week's material

- **Overview:** a broad picture of where the week's topic is headed

- **Engage:** some weeks include an opportunity for participants to start personalizing the information right away

- **Reflect and Discuss:** questions for participants to engage with the material and with each other (some sessions include a second set of questions for additional engagement and discussion)

- **Journey Deeper:** additional teaching on the week's topic

- **Journey On:** suggestions for participants to apply the work between gatherings

FOR GROUP LEADERS

I am so grateful for your willingness to lead a group through this study guide. I have found that although a leadership position requires a larger commitment, there is often a gift to be found in the role. It's my prayer that this will be true for you.

You'll find each chapter in this study guide generally follows the same format. You are surely welcome to work your way through each chapter however you see fit, but I have structured the chapters imagining that groups will want to gather for about an hour or so:

Check In: approximately ten to fifteen minutes

Overview, Engage, Reflect and Discuss: approximately fifteen to twenty minutes

Journey Deeper, Reflect and Discuss: approximately fifteen to twenty minutes

Journey On: approximately five to ten minutes

Keep in mind that Enneagram work is inherently very personal. So as you set the table for your group to enter into this transformational work, I would encourage you to be gentle but firm in naming and encouraging some group norms for your time together. There are a number of excellent resources for creating grace-filled, honest environments for groups, but as we consider this study guide in particular I would encourage you to shape your gatherings around the Four Mantras. These mantras come from Angeles Arrien and are found in her book *The Four-Fold Way*. I have found them to be helpful in so many situations, and I believe they provide a framework for entering into this work together. Here's my summary of them:

1. Show up: It's important to be there for group work—physically present in the room, of course, but it's also important to be engaged mentally and spiritually.

2. Pay attention: In group settings, it's important to pay attention to what others are sharing. It's just as important, though, to pay attention to what is happening within ourselves.

3. Tell the truth: It's important to tell the truth to ourselves and to others.

4. Don't get attached to the results: Transformation is rarely linear and happens even less often according to our timetable. The journey is significantly more important than the destination.

As a last reminder, the purpose of these gatherings is not to problem solve. This study guide is set up for participants to *learn about* other people, not to "help" other people be different. So much of the goodness of spiritual work in community comes from the unique opportunity to be with other people—people who represent all nine ways of seeing the world, and whose goal is being healthier themselves. This solitary work cannot be done alone, but it also cannot be done on behalf of others.

May your time together be a gift and a blessing, and may this study guide be an offering of grace—grace for yourself and grace for the people you encounter as you journey toward wholeness.

1

SAFEGUARDING OUR SOULS

Even when there is much to do, we must first guard our souls.

THE JOURNEY TOWARD WHOLENESS

READ

The Journey Toward Wholeness part one, "Triads: Naming and Managing Your Dominant Center of Intelligence"

CHECK IN

Welcome! I'm so glad that you have chosen to spend some more intentional time working through the concepts presented in *The Journey Toward Wholeness*. I'm hopeful that this offering will give you the opportunity to explore the essence of who you are—*essence* referring to who we are at our core, our spiritual being, uniquely created by God. Moving on from there, you can begin to allow pieces of your false personality to fall away.

The work of the Enneagram is primarily soul work, and soul work is never one and done. While we might wish for instant change or quick fixes, those just aren't real choices for transformational work. Instead, there is the offer of a lifetime journey. Once we begin the spiritual journey there isn't an end point during this lifetime, just an invitation to keep journeying.

But culture not only encourages our desire for immediacy, it also most often grants it. We can have what we want *right now*: credit cards offer us the opportunity to make home purchases we can't currently afford. We read the CliffsNotes of great literature instead of reading the whole book. And watching the latest movie no longer takes a trip to the theater because it can appear instantly in our living room.

I think of wholeness in terms of wholistic living, not a place where we arrive. In other words, wholeness itself is a journey. In fact, wholeness sets the table for all transformative moments, and transformative moments increase our understanding of wholeness.

We often want to control our own transformative experience, but that desire actually negates a true understanding of transformation. We have some control when we want to change something, and little or none when it comes to an opportunity for transformation. Unfortunately, you just can't write "wholeness" on your to-do list for Thursday!

Because we seek immediate gratification we're losing the understanding of what it's like to even be on the journey. We have a plan for almost everything, but when it comes to the spiritual journey, we're nomads. We never get "there." We just keep journeying toward wholeness.

Your triad is determined by your first response when you encounter information or situations.

Of course, there is great value in unpacking these pages by yourself, but I am hopeful that you'll go through this workbook with a trusted friend or small group. A partner or group can help keep you accountable to doing your work. Some Enneagram numbers might be tempted to speed-read their way through the book so that they can "finish." Others might have sincere intentions of methodically working through the information but never quite make it past the first few pages. Somewhere in the middle is ideal—thoughtfully engaging with the material—and a friend or group will help keep you on track.

Let's start by taking some time to learn about the person or people you'll be going through this workbook with. If you're planning to embark on this journey with a spouse or sibling, you can probably skip the first question, but leave room to be curious and surprised. You never know what you might learn!

- Share your name, Enneagram number, and how long you've been doing Enneagram work.

- Share why you are interested in embarking on this journey now.

- Share any hopes or goals you have for this journey together.

OVERVIEW

Triads are the foundational grouping of the Enneagram, and they are determined by which Center of Intelligence is primary, or dominant, for each of us: the Heart, Head, or Gut Triad.

THE ENNEAGRAM CENTERS OF INTELLIGENCE AND STANCES

NUMBER	TRIAD	STANCE	PREFERRED AND DOMINANT CENTER	SUPPORT CENTER	REPRESSED CENTER
One	Gut	Dependent	Doing	Feeling	Thinking
Two	Heart	Dependent	Feeling	Doing	Thinking
Three	Heart	Aggressive	Feeling	Thinking / Doing* Doing / Thinking	Feeling
Four	Heart	Withdrawing	Feeling	Thinking	Doing
Five	Head	Withdrawing	Thinking	Feeling	Doing
Six	Head	Dependent	Thinking	Feeling / Doing Doing / Feeling	Thinking
Seven	Head	Aggressive	Thinking	Doing	Feeling
Eight	Gut	Aggressive	Doing	Thinking	Feeling
Nine	Gut	Withdrawing	Doing	Thinking / Feeling Feeling / Thinking	Doing

*The core numbers Three, Six, and Nine are both dominant and repressed in the same Center of Intelligence. In the support center, one will lead, the other will follow.

HEART (TWO, THREE, FOUR)

■ First response to life: What do I feel?

■ Shame is just below the surface

■ Characterized by love, empathy, connection, loss, and pain

■ Generally search for both love and affirmation outside of themselves

HEAD (FIVE, SIX, SEVEN)

■ First response to life: What do I think?

■ Fear is just below the surface

■ Logical and rational; they choose reasoning over emotions and judgment over reacting

■ Like to gather and sort information; usually very knowledgeable about things and ideas that interest them

GUT (EIGHT, NINE, ONE)

■ First response to life: What will I do?

■ Anger is just below the surface

■ Usually busy, which suits them because they have lots of vitality and are very determined—often to the point of being stubborn

■ Pulled to both outer world and inner world, focusing on one and then the other

REFLECT AND DISCUSS

1. What resonates with you about your triad?

2. Describe a time, either earlier today or earlier this week, when you were presented with a situation or idea and responded from your primary Center of Intelligence.

3. What surprises you the most about how people in other triads respond to the world?

JOURNEY DEEPER

I'll never forget where I was when I was first introduced to the concept that I could grow my soul. I had been a part of wonderful faith communities throughout my life, but somehow I had never gotten the idea that I could contribute to growing my soul. I had no idea that I had agency in my own development. As I have lived more fully into that idea over the decades, I have added another idea: I believe I am also responsible for safeguarding my soul.

Safeguarding is a kind of care for yourself and your own soul. It isn't attached to a list of hard and fast rules. It isn't as simple as don't have sex before marriage or do wear nice clothes to worship on Sunday. Instead, it has to do with recognizing how you're put together—how you take in the information that the world or your culture offers to you. Safeguarding your soul is about awareness and discernment. It's about knowing the people and ideas that may influence you or your thinking in some way.

We are living in a world that is filled with visual and verbal impressions. If you aren't mindful, these impressions that often come quickly and from all sides are only received and interpreted by your primary or dominant Center of Intelligence. Unfortunately, that means you only are only seeing and experiencing one-third of what's happening.

As you might know, I learned the Enneagram from Father Richard Rohr. He has been a kind and gracious friend and mentor to Joe and me for many years, so I have vivid memories surrounding the first time I strongly disagreed with something Father Rohr was teaching. As an Enneagram Two, I filter most information through the lens of my feelings. One result is that I cannot take in information without considering how it will affect the relationships in my life. As Father Rohr taught, I thought to myself, "Who am I to disagree with him?" And from there I began to wonder how it might affect our relationship for me to disagree with what he was saying.

Ultimately, giving myself permission to think independently became a major step in learning to safeguard my soul. Recognizing that I can listen to others and still respectfully disagree with them was key. Father Rohr is still a great friend of ours, but over the years I have disagreed with some of his thinking. To his credit, he has welcomed it every time.

Safeguarding your soul might include things like recognizing that double dates with a couple who constantly fights could have a negative influence on your marriage. It might mean that adult children need to safeguard themselves from intrusive, overactive parenting. It could include knowing which books, music, or movies offer something valuable for your life, and which ones can have the opposite effect. If this is a new concept for you, you might start with acknowledging which one of the Centers of Intelligence you use when receiving information—thinking, feeling or doing—and then begin to consider whether or not you feel differently if you use all three.

> **Soul work is best done in the context of community.**

When Joe was much younger, still a priest in the Catholic church, he attended a large, multicity worship gathering. As the evening progressed a woman in front of Joe's group turned around and said, "God told me to pray over you," speaking only to Joe. "Oh," Joe replied. "Oh, no thank you." Joe's eyes still get wide when he tells that story today. "I didn't even know her!" he'll say. "Who was she?" Joe was safeguarding his soul.

Taking care of your soul can look different for each Enneagram number. Here's a list of suggested ideas for each type to help you start thinking about how you might safeguard your soul:

1s Safeguarding your soul includes naming your inner, critical voice in order to deflect the things that aren't true.

2s Safeguarding your soul includes not making assumptions in relationships about people who are not relational in the same way you are.

3s Safeguarding your soul includes allowing yourself to be more authentic.

4s Safeguarding your soul includes not asking yourself to be any more or any less.

5s Safeguarding your soul includes allowing a scarcity mentality to fall away.

6s Safeguarding your soul includes trusting yourself.

7s Safeguarding your soul includes allowing for a full range of feelings, not just the happy half.

8s Safeguarding your soul means learning to think before you act or react.

9s Safeguarding your soul includes doing what is yours to do, and recognizing that later is not a point in time.

REFLECT AND DISCUSS

1. What does safeguarding your soul mean to you?

2. How do you react to the prompt for your number above?

3. Share an example of something you have done to safeguard your soul.

JOURNEY ON

Safeguarding our soul is active not passive work. Before you gather for session two, make a commitment to follow through on the prompt for your triad below:

Heart Triad. Pay attention to your own feelings and emotions. This could be a one-time coffee date with yourself and a journal, or you could place a pad of paper on your nightstand and write down a feeling or emotion each night before bed. Or you could check in with your feelings and emotions during your afternoon walk. Be aware as you do this good work that fulfilling others' expectations provides the approval you seek, but it's a poor substitute for more intimate desires.

Head Triad. Pay attention to how much of your life is driven by fear. Commit to (at least) a daily check-in with yourself to notice the motivation for the choices you've made. Each day, identify a couple of choices you made and consider what role, if any, fear played in your decision. Did that choice lead you into wholeness or encourage you to shrink back? It is always your option to connect with your soul in ways that enlarge rather than diminish the goodness of who you are.

Gut Triad. Pay attention to the relationship between what you are doing (or not doing) and other people. What did I do that wasn't mine to do? What was mine to do that I didn't do? What did I do that could be perceived by someone else as criticism? When did I use doing as a substitute for feeling or thinking? The reality is that often when people in the Gut Triad don't have the energy for what needs to be done, they do something else as a substitute. But that's not helpful because when you finish, you're still tired and the task is still not done.

2

MANAGING OUR DOMINANT CENTERS

It is generally and universally accepted by the world's philosophies and religions that human beings are born with three native intelligences: thinking, feeling, and doing. . . . These Centers of Intelligence, as the Enneagram names them, are our natural resources, and if we can learn to use each one for its intended purpose, the result will be a more balanced approach to life.

THE JOURNEY TOWARD WHOLENESS

READ

The Journey Toward Wholeness part one, "Triads: Naming and Managing Your Dominant Center of Intelligence"

CHECK IN

Welcome back! Before we dive in this week, take a few minutes to share your observations from last week's assignment.

- What was it like to really pay attention to your feelings, thoughts, or activities?

- Did anything surprise you? If so, what?

Remember, the more we're able to be open and honest about the gifts and graces that are part of our unique and valuable way of being in the world, the more we will be able to honor and celebrate the unique gifts and goodness in others.

OVERVIEW

This week we'll continue to focus on the dominant Center of Intelligence. One of the things I'm careful to teach in any Enneagram workshop is this: *you can't change how you see, but you can change what you do with how you see.* The same holds true for Centers of Intelligence. You can't change the Center of Intelligence that is dominant for you, but you can change what you do in relation to that center. I refer to that as managing your dominant center.

The work of balancing our Centers of Intelligence is the work of a lifetime. Remember, the preferred center sees only one-third of what is being experienced, and it treats both the focus and response of the two other centers as unimportant. The goal is to learn to use each of the centers—thinking, feeling, and doing—for its own purpose.

Enneagram wisdom offers a structured and organized way of using the three centers: Feeling is for acknowledging feelings, ours and others, and for awareness of needs and agendas, ours and others. Thinking is for gathering and sorting information, for analyzing and making plans. Doing is for accomplishing and pleasure seeking. Each are important and necessary if we want to live full, holistic lives.

ENGAGE

Take a look at the chart below and add some more of your own examples.

Appropriate Uses of Each Center of Intelligence

FEELING
- Building and maintaining relationships
- Awareness of how other people are responding to you
- Compassion in responding to others
-
-

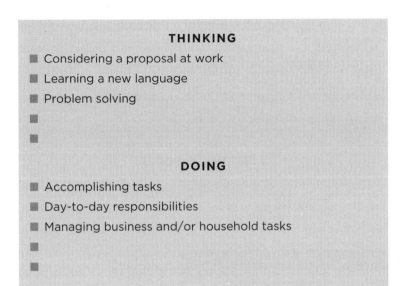

THINKING

■ Considering a proposal at work

■ Learning a new language

■ Problem solving

■

■

DOING

■ Accomplishing tasks

■ Day-to-day responsibilities

■ Managing business and/or household tasks

■

■

It can be easy to slip into judgmental observations when others are not using what you perceive as the appropriate Center of Intelligence for a situation. This might sound like, "How can she be so stoic at a funeral? Didn't she care that her friend died?" or "It's great that he handles the laundry, but I wish we spent more time connecting as a couple instead of just managing the same household." We are often impatient with people who don't share our dominant center.

REFLECT AND DISCUSS

Take a few moments to answer and then discuss the following questions with your journey partner or group:

1. Identify one of the examples you added to the list for each center and explain your reason for including it.

2. What surprises you about what other people added?

3. Can you think of a time in the last week or so that your dominant center showed up, took the lead, and you followed by responding to a situation with either feeling, thinking, or doing?

4. When has your dominant Center of Intelligence caused you trouble? (Perhaps it was a time when you overused your dominant center instead of the Center of Intelligence needed for the situation.)

5. Describe what happened in an interpersonal relationship when different centers caused friction.

JOURNEY DEEPER

When you don't do the work to manage your dominant Center of Intelligence, you have a very limited view of life. It's important to remember that when you use one center, you only see one-third of what's happening. It's hard to commit to the work of using all three centers, so we all use the same excuse: "I've made it this far using only two of the three centers and I'm doing fairly well." It requires a lot of nonjudgmental (but honest)

> Those who make up the Feeling Triad are pulled to the outer world where they try to control their environment by ordering other people and activities.

self-observation to be able to acknowledge the loss that results from over-using one center, while under-utilizing the second, and for the most part ignoring the third.

It might be helpful to think of the three centers of intelligence as three natural elements: water, fire, and air. You wouldn't consider trying to make it through life primarily relying on only one element. You would miss so much if you did! In the same way, you wouldn't expect any element to do the work of another. Each element has its own place and cannot substitute for another. The same is true of our natural resources of thinking, feeling, and doing.

Early in our marriage, Joe and I attended a workshop that centered around financial stewardship. Many of the teachings were reminders of the basics: spend less than you earn, give generously, and save. But I've never forgotten one of the exercises and I think it's because it so clearly identified my dominant center. The presenter asked us all to get out our check registers. (For the young ones: this was before debit cards, when we used to write checks and then record deposits and purchases so we wouldn't overdraw our account.)

As participants, we were asked to look at our checkbooks and categorize our spending as either necessary (rent, groceries, bills, etc.) or extraneous. Raising four children on a pastor's salary, Joe and I had been through the record of our spending many times. But this time we had an added assignment—to consider our motivation behind any unplanned purchases.

As we discussed the reasons for any spending that was not included in our monthly budget, and while questioning the motivation behind any of my "extra" spending, I discovered that these purchases all had one thing in common: my feelings. It was easy for me to justify those purchases as I explained to Joe the feelings that I had about what I bought, and for whom. In my mind I knew we didn't need more Girl Scout cookies, but my heart thought we should buy some

> **Those who are in the Thinking Triad look for safety by trying to control their inner world.**

from each of the girls in our church, not just one or two. Thankfully, this teaching doesn't only apply to those of us who are feeling dominant. Perhaps you've said to a friend, "I'm so glad you're doing well. I thought about coming by after your surgery." The reality is that thinking about taking someone a casserole doesn't really count. Those of us who are thinking dominant will have to access the doing Center of Intelligence as well to care for that friend.

Like learning any new skill, your first attempts at managing your dominant center might feel awkward or uncomfortable, and that's okay. The truth is if you are going to commit to a journey toward wholeness and transformation, then it stands to reason that you're going to need to use all three Centers of Intelligence. And you won't be successful if you don't begin by learning to manage the center that is dominant.

REFLECT AND DISCUSS

1. Think through your recent purchases. What are some trends in your spending—not what you purchase, but why you make those purchases?

2. What transaction would you undo or redo if you could?

3. Take a few moments to read through the "Try This" section at the end of each Enneagram number's chapter in the first part of *The Journey Toward Wholeness*. These sections list a number of practices for managing your feeling, thinking, or doing.

   a. Name the things on the list that make you the most uncomfortable, and then talk about why.

   b. When you look at the list for your number, what are your feelings?

   c. What are your thoughts?

   d. What does that list make you want to do?

JOURNEY ON

Take a moment to read through the suggested practices for your number one more time and choose one that you will commit to for the coming week. Share that practice with someone in your group and listen as they share the practice they've chosen to commit to for the week. The whole purpose of this exercise is accountability.

It's surprising how much more we accomplish if we share our intention with someone else. And, of course, if you aren't able to complete the assignment, it's really nice to receive understanding and grace from that same person.

Some Enneagram numbers might be tempted to choose more than one practice to attempt for this week. One is plenty. Remember, we're on a journey, and it's not a sprint. As Pastor Eugene Peterson would say, this is a long obedience in the same direction.

Other Enneagram types might be tempted to defer choosing a practice until they have more time to think about it or consider their plans for the week. It's okay to change your mind later, but it would be good to go ahead and make a decision now and share that with your partner or group.

> If you are in the Doing Triad, you're probably pulled to both the inner and the outer world, focusing on one and then the other. You want control over both.

3

THE HIGH SIDE
OF STRESS

*When we encounter the inevitable stresses of life,
whatever their cause, our initial reaction is to exaggerate
our normal behavior. . . . When excessive behavior is
still unsuccessful, we intuitively draw on the resources of
another number in order to feel stronger. That number
is our stress number.*

THE JOURNEY TOWARD WHOLENESS

READ

The Journey Toward Wholeness part one, "Triads: Naming and Managing Your Dominant Center of Intelligence"

CHECK IN

I'm so glad you're back this week. As you gather, take some time to share your experience in relation to the practice you chose to commit to for the week.

- What did you notice about yourself?
- Were you surprised by anything?
- What was easy? Difficult?

OVERVIEW

This week we'll be exploring the movement around the Enneagram, focusing on the lines that connect us to our stress and security numbers. If you're not positive about which numbers you are connected to on the Enneagram, take a moment to be sure. Check out the diagram of the Enneagram below.

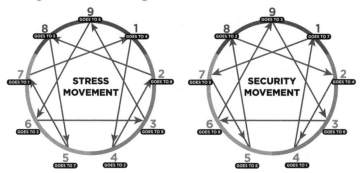

Start with your Enneagram number and go *with* the arrow to your stress number. Then beginning with your number again, go *against* the arrow to the number you go to in Security. Jot them down here for reference:

My Enneagram number: _____

My stress number: _____

My security number: _____

Other very wise Enneagram teachers have used different words to describe the movements that I refer to as *stress* and *security*. Some refer to these as moves toward integration and disintegration, or as moves toward consolation and disconsolation. All of these are good representations of the moves, and I would encourage you to use the words that best represent your way of thinking and offer you the most comfort. I prefer stress and security, so I will continue to use those.

These moves are a significant element of Enneagram wisdom but they're kind of hard to explain. As I continue to try to find just the right words for teaching about the stress and security moves, I find that sometimes it just helps to spend some time answering questions.

Here are a few that I regularly hear when I'm teaching about the stress and security moves.

Stress Number FAQs

■ How do I get to my stress number?

You move to your stress number intuitively, but once you know the Enneagram you can choose to access the same behavior intentionally.

■ When I'm stressed, does my motivation change?

No. You don't take on the motivations of the stress number. Your core Enneagram number is determined by your motivation and that doesn't change.

■ What about time orientation? Does that change in stress?

No. You don't take on the time orientation of the stress number.

■ What about wings—do I take on the wings of my stress number?

No again. You don't add the wings of your stress number.

■ How much stress are you talking about? Can I be in stress for years? Or what about moments?

Yes to both. Stress can be long-term—like losing a job without a replacement on the horizon, or the unexpected death of a loved one; or short-term—like a coworker who frustrates you, or a puppy that won't stop chewing shoes.

■ What about trauma?

Although trauma is stress producing, trauma and stress are two different things. My understanding of the Enneagram is that trauma doesn't change your core Enneagram number.

ENGAGE

The key to using your stress number for good is recognizing when you're behaving badly in your own number. To help you understand what I mean by "behaving badly," I've listed a few examples for each number. The most helpful thing you can do is start to recognize your own movement from healthy through average into unhealthy. After you read these examples below of how each number behaves badly (and please don't miss this: each number does indeed behave badly), fill in the blanks with behavior you recognize in yourself when you move from healthy through average and into unhealthy space.

1s

- Increasingly critical of yourself and others
- More dualistic thinking—everything is right or wrong, good or bad
- Feeling like it's up to you, and only you, to improve everything from organizing the spice drawer to addressing a social justice issue
-

2s

- Being overly friendly and lost in people-pleasing
- Giving that is not altruistic
- Anticipating and meeting the needs of others for manipulative reasons
-

3s

- "Spinning" facts or stories to put yourself in the best light
- Becoming overly concerned with image

■ Prioritizing efficiency or goals over human relationships
■

4s

■ Becoming self-absorbed and moody
■ Allowing made-up scenarios to take the place of real life and its messiness
■ Self-contempt
■

5s

■ Detaching from the outer world in order give more energy to thinking and conceptualizing
■ Increased sarcasm and cynicism
■ Antagonistic toward anything that is perceived as a threat to your preferred agenda
■

6s

■ Increasing need for alliances and us-versus-them thinking
■ Passive-aggressive behavior
■ Increased suspicion
■

7s

■ Inability to focus or complete a task
■ Exaggerated or hyperbolic speech and storytelling
■ Frenetic activity, perpetual motion
■

8s

■ Increasing importance on self-reliance and independence

■ Combative or confrontational

■ Dominating environment and relationships

■

9s

■ Accommodating and merging

■ Pushing against social and non-work-related expectations

■ Withdrawn and quiet

■

REFLECT AND DISCUSS

1. Do the given examples ring true?

2. What examples did you add to your own Enneagram number? Why? (If there is anyone else in your group who shares your number, please take the opportunity to compare your observations.)

3. Can you think of a story to share from your own life when you weren't behaving at your best?

JOURNEY DEEPER

Teaching about the move to our stress numbers is a place where I break with traditional Enneagram teaching. Historically, Enneagram teaching taught us that in stress, we move down from healthy into average and then to unhealthy in our own number, and then make the lateral move to the unhealthy behaviors of our stress number. In other words, we move from the low side of our number to the low side of our stress number.

I've struggled with this as long as I've known the Enneagram because in my experience and understanding, the Enneagram is always helpful. And it is not at all helpful for me, as a Two, to move to the unhealthy side of Eight. In fact, that usually makes a situation worse! As I've done my own work over the past fifteen or twenty years, while talking with the people around me and asking lots of questions when I'm teaching, I have grown in my conviction that you can learn enough about your stress number to access its highest and best behaviors. In fact, with some disciplined awareness and honest self-observation, we can all learn to choose behavior from the high, healthy side of our stress numbers *before* we give in to behaving badly in our own number. This move is, for me, one of the greatest gifts of the Enneagram.

After my mom died, our entire extended family gathered at her home in the small Texas panhandle town where she spent more than sixty years of her life. She had long since downsized from the large two-story house I was raised in, choosing a small, single-story house that better suited her needs. As we arrived—one family after another, my brothers and their spouses, their children who had children, and Joe and me along with our crew, filling the house seemingly from corner to corner—the stress was palpable, especially among the adults. The kids were acting as kids do, excited to see their cousins and aware that the atmosphere was crackling. My grief increased along with the confusion and the noise until I lost it and started yelling at anyone who was younger than me, insisting on some order and "respect." When I was out of energy and breath, I went to my mom's room and closed the door.

> A determining factor in using your stress number for good is recognizing when you're behaving badly in your own number.

My oldest daughter, Joey, an Enneagram Eight, let me catch my breath and then came into the room and sat down in front of me. "Grandma would never say no to anything they're doing," she said. "It's still her house and they're just being kids. She would love that they're here and that we're all together."

I'll never forget that moment because Joey was exactly right. It was a defining moment in my journey to understand stress and the Enneagram because it was then that I began to think there was no excuse for my behavior. I began to explore the idea of acting more like Joey in the high, healthy side of her Eightness. Weeks later I journaled that "perhaps it could be possible to have good boundaries and express what I needed, while grieving the loss of my mom, while also honoring her and how she would have been in her own home."

> The key to this type of Enneagram work is nonjudgmental self-observation.

Looking back I feel sure that only Joey, the solitary Eight in our family, could have spoken that truth to me at that moment on that day. Joey was self-aware enough by then to know her own range of Eight behavior. From that place she offered me a different way of seeing and responding. Because our relationship was healthy, because of the Enneagram work she had done, and because I was willing to listen to a hard truth from someone whose love I could trust, things changed for our whole family that day. I'm still so thankful.

REFLECT AND DISCUSS

1. As you learn about the healthy side of your stress number, what behaviors seem the most foreign to you?

2. What behaviors associated with your stress number seem like they have the most to offer you in times of stress?

3. Is there anyone in your group whose Enneagram type is your stress number?

   a. If so, spend ten to fifteen minutes talking to them about what it is like to be healthy in their number.

   b. If not, do you know anyone else in your life who is that number that you can connect with? Does anyone in your group know someone they could introduce you to?

JOURNEY ON

Over the next week, commit to paying attention to your moves away from and toward your number on the Enneagram. And pay special attention to your behavior as you move up and down—from healthy, down through average to unhealthy, and then hopefully back up again. What behavior can you name that is the best of you? And what is the worst?

The key to this type of Enneagram work is nonjudgmental self-observation. If you judge or shame yourself, then you defend yourself and you have to start over one more time. But if you can just observe with no judgment and no excuses, then you can begin to allow unhealthy behavior to simply fall away. Be clear: you can't *make it go away;* you have to learn to allow it to fall away. It's tricky but it is worth the work.

If you're really brave, consider asking someone who knows you well to help with this assignment. While we don't often like to admit it, there's a good chance that the people who love us know how healthy (or unhealthy) we are in any given moment.

4

STANCES

We achieve balance by appropriately using
all three Centers of Intelligence.

THE JOURNEY TOWARD WHOLENESS

READ

The Journey Toward Wholeness part two, "Stances: Naming and Managing Your Repressed Center of Intelligence"

CHECK IN

I'm so glad you're here this week. Before we dive into stances, let's look back at our discussion about stress from last week.

- What did you learn from your nonjudgmental self-observation?

- When were you able to observe yourself in healthy space? When were you able to observe yourself moving down into unhealthy space?

It would be great if you are willing to share a story or two with your partner or group.

OVERVIEW

I often joke that my teaching schedule is almost always full because my teaching is about everyone's favorite subject: *themselves*! I'm thankful for the gift it is for me to spend time helping people get to know themselves in new ways. And thanks to the Enneagram I get to speak some wisdom into conversations about how to change habitual behavior that doesn't serve them well. It's good for them and so good for those they love.

Occasionally, though, people just aren't ready to hear something about themselves that comes as a surprise, so when I teach stances, I often get some pushback. The truth is, it's not easy to learn that you are repressed in one of the three Centers of Intelligence.

In fact, one time when I was teaching a stances workshop at the Micah Center, our ministry center, a woman came up to me during a break. She had been listening and engaged throughout the morning, but when she started moving toward me, I was aware that she had packed up the handouts and her journal, and her keys were in her hand. Hoping she hadn't learned of some sort of family emergency, I asked if she was okay. "I really thought you had something valuable here in the Enneagram," she replied, shaking her head, "but then you got to all of that talk about repressed thinking. I am a One on the Enneagram and I am sure of that! And I do not have repressed thinking and I am sure of that!" And with that, she walked out the door.

> Each of us, according to our Enneagram stance, have one Center of Intelligence that is unproductive, underused, underdeveloped, unfamiliar, or protected.

In fairness, when it comes to the teaching that we are repressed in either our thinking, feeling, or doing, I think that's how we'd all like to respond. After all, we've done a pretty good job of making our way in the world up to now, so it can be unsettling or even offensive to hear that we either don't think, don't feel, or don't do. Of course, that's an exaggeration, but that's how many people hear the teaching about stances for the first time. Offensive or not, though, it's the truth.

Each of us, according to our Enneagram stance, has one Center of Intelligence that is unproductive, underused, underdeveloped, unfamiliar, or protected (I thought I'd give you a number of alternative options in case you don't like *repressed*).

It just takes some time for people to recognize and acknowledge their repressed center. And that's okay. The next step is even more demanding

> Just wrap your arms around all of who you are and keep moving.

because learning to appropriately use this repressed center will be our life-long work. It's difficult work because this is the center we use the least effectively, or simply use the least, and that reality is most apparent in our personal lives.

WITHDRAWING STANCE (FOUR, FIVE, NINE)

NUMBER	TRIAD	STANCE	PREFERRED AND DOMINANT CENTER	SUPPORT CENTER	REPRESSED CENTER
Four	Heart	Withdrawing	Feeling	Thinking	Doing
Five	Head	Withdrawing	Thinking	Feeling	Doing
Nine	Gut	Withdrawing	Doing	Thinking / Feeling Feeling / Thinking	Doing

- Repressed doing
- Move away from other people
- Accustomed to focusing inward
- Have an independent point of view
- Retreat into themselves
- Depend on their own strength to get through
- Rely on thinking and feeling
- Appreciate intricacy

AGGRESSIVE STANCE (THREE, SEVEN, EIGHT)

NUMBER	TRIAD	STANCE	PREFERRED AND DOMINANT CENTER	SUPPORT CENTER	REPRESSED CENTER
Three	Heart	Aggressive	Feeling	Thinking / Doing Doing / Thinking	Feeling
Seven	Head	Aggressive	Thinking	Doing	Feeling
Eight	Gut	Aggressive	Doing	Thinking	Feeling

- Repressed feeling
- Stand independently from other people
- Accustomed to orienting toward their own ideas and actions
- Think and do
- Feel free to do what they want or need to do
- Think they can shape the world according to their image of it

DEPENDENT STANCE (ONE, TWO, SIX)

NUMBER	TRIAD	STANCE	PREFERRED AND DOMINANT CENTER	SUPPORT CENTER	REPRESSED CENTER
One	Gut	Dependent	Doing	Feeling	Thinking
Two	Heart	Dependent	Feeling	Doing	Thinking
Six	Head	Dependent	Thinking	Feeling / Doing Doing / Feeling	Thinking

- Repressed thinking
- Move toward other people
- Accustomed to responding to people and situations
- Simply stated: they see a need and try to fill it
- Feel responsible for making things better
- The immediate situation determines their agenda

REFLECT AND DISCUSS

1. What was your first reaction when you learned about stances?

2. Can you recognize when you move toward others, away from others, or stand independently?

3. I offer a number of other synonyms for the traditional "repressed" Enneagram teaching: unproductive, underused, underdeveloped, unfamiliar, or protected. Which word resonates with you? Why?

4. Which of the characteristics listed about your stance do you see most clearly in your own life?

5. What is most surprising to you about how other stances move through the world?

ENGAGE

The three Centers of Intelligence play out in each of our lives, informing our decisions and reactions an infinite number of times throughout the day. Our dominant center (triad) and our repressed center (stance) show themselves in our actions and responses. On your own, read through these case studies and the question that follows. Then share your response and talk through the remaining questions with the others in your group.

Case Study 1: The Difficult Student

Imagine that you're a high school teacher who offered a few tutoring sessions for students who need extra help before tomorrow's exam. Just before lunch, a difficult student who hasn't attended any of the optional tutoring sessions asks you for help. You have an open period this afternoon, but your plan was to use that time to work on grades so you wouldn't have to take that work home.

Case Study 2: The Tense Funeral

A number of years ago, my husband, Joe, was the officiant for a funeral. Every death is tragic, but since this man was young and newly married, emotions were running high. He and his wife had been in the United States for a few years, but much of his extended family lived overseas in their home country.

After the funeral, the family proceeded to the cemetery for the graveside service. Upon arriving at the grave, the funeral directors found that they were unable to turn off the hearse. The pall bearers removed the casket from the back of the hearse just as the driver popped the hood in the front and began to fiddle with the whining engine.

The family's burial plot was near the back of the cemetery, just across the fence from a large apartment complex. The newly widowed wife was seated at one end of the front row while the grieving mother was seated at the other end. These two had largely ignored each other throughout the funeral but now whisper-fought throughout the graveside prayers. Those gathered learned that while the wife wanted her husband buried in that cemetery, his mother felt strongly that he should rest in the earth of his home country.

As Joe prayed over the sound of the hearse's still whining engine, he and others heard shouting. It soon became obvious that a couple in one of the apartments was having a really big fight. The shouting got louder and louder, leading up to the gunshot that commanded the attention of everyone.

The gunshot was the last straw for the brother of the deceased, who stood up, and while attempting to pick up the coffin, declared to his mother that he would carry the coffin home!

> *For each of these situations, how would you have responded? Why?*

REFLECT AND DISCUSS

For each of these examples, answer the following questions:

1. How can you see your Centers of Intelligence playing out in your answer?

   a. How did feelings affect your response?

   b. Thinking?

   c. Doing?

2. What is surprising to you about how other people imagine they would have responded?

JOURNEY DEEPER

Enneagram stances can be a tricky concept for all of us, but even more so for the core Enneagram numbers: Three, Six, and Nine. These Enneagram types make up the central triangle on the Enneagram and are the anchor numbers in each of their triads. Each of these three core numbers is dominant and repressed in the same center.

Threes are both feeling dominant (Heart Triad) and feeling repressed (Aggressive Stance). This means that while they take in information using feeling, they set feelings aside almost immediately and instead use thinking and doing to make their way moving forward. Threes set goals and then they reach them, only to start the pattern all over again. They are focused on efficiency and problem solving. They find feelings to be messy and unpredictable, and they block efficiency and effectiveness, so Threes don't like to deal with them for any extended period of time.

Sixes are both thinking dominant (Head Triad) and thinking repressed (Dependent Stance). This means that while they take in information using productive thinking, they don't include thinking when trying to make sense of the information they have received. Sixes often find it difficult to trust themselves, so they tend to rely on the thinking of experts and other proven systems for answers. Meanwhile they make plans for caring for themselves and those they love in case of some unexpected event.

Nines are both doing dominant (Gut Triad) and doing repressed (Withdrawing Stance). This means they take in information with what needs to be done, but in responding it doesn't occur to them that they should be the one to do it. I teach that Nines walk into a room and see what needs to be done (a lightbulb changed, a lonely person greeted, an event planned) and think, "Someone should handle that." To all the Nines I say, *"What about you? Could you be the someone?"*

JOURNEY ON

At regular intervals throughout your day this week, commit to asking yourself:

What am I thinking? (Dependent Stance)

What am I doing? (Withdrawing Stance)

What am I feeling? (Aggressive Stance)

As we discussed last week, a lot of transformative Enneagram work is based on nonjudgmental self-observation, so don't be too hard on yourself if your answer is "nothing." Don't waste your time or energy chiding yourself for your nonproductive Center of Intelligence. Just wrap your arms around all of who you are and keep moving. And know that every time you are aware enough to bring up your repressed center, you are one step closer to wholeness than you were before. And you can make it along this entire journey one good step after another.

5

BRINGING UP THE REPRESSED CENTER

Developing the repressed center becomes the great challenge of Enneagram work. And it is work you will need to do for the rest of your life. But it's worth it. It is transformational and creates spiritual vitality, and it truly makes all the difference.

THE JOURNEY TOWARD WHOLENESS

READ

The Journey Toward Wholeness part two, "Stances: Naming and Managing Your Repressed Center of Intelligence"

CHECK IN

Welcome back! This week, we'll continue our deep dive into Enneagram stances by talking about how to bring up your repressed Center of Intelligence. Before we get into the specifics, take some time to share your experiences from the last week with your group.

- How often were you able to ask yourself what you were thinking, feeling, or doing?

- How did you remind yourself to be aware of this throughout the day?

- What patterns did you notice in yourself?

OVERVIEW

Bringing up your repressed Center of Intelligence is the work of a lifetime. It's hard work, though, and I often find that when people push against the idea that they have a repressed center it's because they genuinely don't believe that it's true. Often, the issue is that they equate the repressed center with the wrong behavior or response. Those in the Withdrawing Stance, doing repressed people, say to me, "I *do* all day long." And that's a logical argument. But what Enneagram stances tell us is that for those in the Withdrawing Stance, their doing isn't always *productive*.

Here's a picture of how being thinking repressed plays out in my own life: I love teaching the Enneagram and often have the privilege of meeting people who share with me that they also want to teach the Enneagram. I believe with all my heart that if everyone understood the Enneagram we would live in a more compassionate world. And I also believe that shallow Enneagram teaching can be harmful, leaving behind

> Developing the repressed center becomes the great challenge of Enneagram work. It is transformational and creates spiritual vitality.

people who use the Enneagram as an excuse for their own bad behavior or use it as a weapon against the behavior of other people.

So when I'm doing my work—when I'm faithful to the discipline of my spiritual practices while working to bring up my thinking—I'm able to say to those people who want to teach the Enneagram, "Wonderful! Here is the list of things I think you should do before you start teaching so you can be faithful to the infinite wisdom of this ancient spiritual tool."

But when I'm in average Two space, at the end of a long day of teaching perhaps, my habitual, patterned response is only to think about the relationship. I want the person in front of me to like me and experience me as helpful. I want the memory to be that we've had a good interaction, so too often I say, "Great! I bet you'll be a wonderful teacher. Have fun!"

Do you see the difference? When I'm in average space, I'm thinking, but I'm relying on feeling and doing to make my way. I'm wondering if the other person likes me and I'm concerned about how I'm being perceived. When I'm able to bring up productive thinking, I'm capable of actually being helpful by providing a real, if difficult, pathway for someone to follow who truly wants to become a good Enneagram teacher.

You should know that when I first told my mentor, Father Richard Rohr, that I wanted to teach the Enneagram, he told me to read every book I could get my hands on. Keep in mind that there were very few Enneagram books available thirty years ago. And then he encouraged me not to talk about it with anyone for five years. It's not lost on me that even before Father Rohr learned about Enneagram stances, he told me to set aside five years to *think*.

> The Enneagram never leaves us without a solution, and the answer to our personality problems almost always begins with finding and learning to maintain balance.

Those in the Aggressive Stance often pay a relational price for repressed feeling, but they don't always know it. Others (those in the Dependent or Withdrawing Stance) often note the lack of relatable or shared feelings from those in the Aggressive Stance. Since aggressive numbers are oriented to the future, they seldom look back, which means they miss opportunities for experiencing and understanding how others react to them. Although those in the Aggressive Stance employ boundaries in order to protect their vulnerability, those same boundaries can also eclipse the vulnerability of others. In other words, it's possible to inadvertently hurt others when they're focused on protecting themselves.

I think it is easier to get away with not thinking or not feeling than to get away with not doing. People have to know you well to catch when you aren't thinking. And generally, an experience with someone who is feeling repressed takes some time to understand. But it's clear to all involved when Fours, Fives, and Nines have failed to *do* something that was theirs to *do*. People tend to be increasingly impatient and judgmental with people who are doing repressed. I'm sorry. But perhaps the silver lining lies in the fact that if those in the Withdrawing Stance get away with less, then they'll have less to repair later on along the journey.

REFLECT AND DISCUSS

1. How do you understand the difference between repressed and productive thinking, feeling, or doing?
2. Can you think of a time when you noticed a lack of thinking, feeling, or doing in someone else? (Be kind as you share!)
3. Now that you can articulate it when you see it in other people, how can you begin to see it in yourself?
4. How can you watch for that repressed center in yourself?
   a. Look for it in real time instead of just looking back.
   b. Are people moving toward you or moving away? Are people following what you're saying or are they distracted?

JOURNEY DEEPER

Management consultant W. Edwards Deming taught that, either intentionally or unintentionally, every system is perfectly designed to get the result that it does. Balancing our Centers of Intelligence offers us the opportunity to move toward different results. If you want something different, if you want to continue your journey toward wholeness, you have to change your habitual, patterned ways of being. You will have to work on bringing up your repressed Center of Intelligence.

Are you tired of

- having someone point out that you didn't do something you said you would?
- people being disappointed in your responses to them?
- finding yourself doing something you don't want to do, for people you don't want to do it for, because you don't want conflict or because you want them to like you?

The answers to all of these can be found in bringing up your repressed center. Here are stories from people who have begun the work of using productive thinking, feeling, and doing.

Bringing Up Feeling

BROCK—THREE

The hardest thing at first about bringing up my repressed center was allowing my feelings to belong as part of me. It took intentional effort to sit with my feelings long enough for them to manifest as things like sadness, loneliness, anger, resentment, fear, etc. I don't think we Threes sit with our feelings long enough to give them descriptions. I might have the first sense of something that is likely a feeling, but I just move right on from it, packing it up and putting it somewhere on a shelf to deal with later.

The long-term work of bringing up my repressed feelings moves beyond naming my feelings to actually sharing those feelings with others. It's one thing to "achieve" being able to name your feelings, but it's totally different to actually tell someone else what that feeling is, especially if it's someone who has wounded you in some way. Sharing my feelings as a Three changes the process of bringing up my repressed center from something I'm good at to something that's good for me and good for those around me.

COURTNEY—SEVEN

Despite the pandemic woes of 2020, I considered myself quite lucky, having a roof over my head, my health, my beloved, pet snuggles, and the distanced social connection of close friends. One day I was on the floor playing with our dogs and my nose got smacked. Hard. Tears instantly welled up, and I felt that desire to cry like you do when your face gets hit, but I held it back. It suddenly occurred to me: "Wait. How long has it been since I had a 'good cry'?"

I realized that in the whole year prior, I might have cried three times. Because it's difficult for me to enter into a good sob session, I decided to take advantage of the physical pain I felt. I went upstairs to my room, shut the door, and brought to mind all of the hurt that I had not yet fully grieved: deaths; loss of work; loss of socialization; the unrelenting return of cancer, yet again, in a young, dear friend. I chose to allow my physical pain to usher me into a necessary emotional grief session. The somatic release afterward was like a huge sigh of relief. None of the situations had changed, but I had. My body had worked through the grief I was suppressing.

I'm very aware that nothing can substitute for deep feeling, but I also know that I must decide to step into it. My natural mode of operation is to avoid pain at all costs, and I am quite good at it. But in order to be whole and to be truly free, I must experience all that life offers—the mountaintops and the valleys.

CAMILLE—INTROVERTED EIGHT

The greatest lessons I have learned about being a feeling repressed, aggressive Eight came through my two years of clinical pastoral education at a local children's hospital. My aggressive Eightness made me good at moving from one trauma to another and doing whatever needed to be done. I was able to move forward with ease. My supervisor quickly challenged me to work toward acknowledging my feelings about the circumstances in which I was ministering. He recognized that I wasn't processing the trauma in front of me or processing the ways in which it intersected with personal trauma.

Numbing the emotions is tricky work because we believe we no longer feel pain, but the pain is always there affecting our behavior regardless of whether or not it is acknowledged. This is not healthy for anyone, and especially not for a chaplain. I was called and commissioned to care for the spiritual and emotional well-being of anyone within the walls of the hospital (including myself). If I was incapable of witnessing to my own feelings, I was incapable of bearing witness to the feelings of those I was called to serve.

MICHELLE—EIGHT

My therapist had me read the book *Adult Children of the Emotionally Immature*. This is a great book because it contains many quick assessments to help one identify the type of emotionally immature parent one has. However, at first I found it extremely difficult to even utilize the assessments.

The assessments should have been super easy except that all of the items on the assessment are describing emotional responses as a child. I was naturally immediately frustrated when looking at the assessments because I could not get even close to any answers. After talking with my therapist, I realized that as a child I didn't deal in the realm of feelings. All of the assessment items were in a language with which I wasn't familiar. So not only did I have to slow myself down in the present, but I also had to slow myself down in the past. I had to *remember*.

I had to remember the little girl who knew deep within her gut that it was not safe to feel. I remembered that it's not that I decided I didn't need feelings and repressed that center, but it's that I had to repress feelings in order to survive. The grownups around me were physically safe but not emotionally safe. That little girl didn't have a safe space to feel all her big feelings without fear of abandonment. Today this grown woman now creates that safe place and welcomes the emotions. Bringing up feeling is helping me unpack my childhood. It's helping me release the layers of personality. The future doesn't have feelings yet, but the past and present do, so that's where I'm trying to live a little more.

Bringing Up Doing

JAMES—FOUR

Bringing up doing has been really good for my relationships. Just as I have to be intentional about my emotions, I have to be very intentional about doing. I find normal, everyday chores to be so boring. But when I add creativity to my intention, I find that I do much better. For example, when I'm cooking dinner, in my mind I'm on a cooking show teaching the viewers how to cook. When I do this, I can stay on task and I'm much more productive.

My dear friend Debbie is a member of the same denomination I belong to. She is aware that the church is making decisions that affect me as a gay man. She told me that the debate in the denomination made her angry and that she thought it was ridiculous. In that moment I was overwhelmed. My feelings were all over the place, but I was able to respond with appropriate intensity to her love for me, calmly talking about both my pain and my hope for the future. It requires a lot of doing for me to manage my dominant center.

DIANA—FIVE

My natural tendency toward relationships is isolation. The friendships I find in the privacy of my home via podcasts and stacks of books hold more safety than some of the friendships I've had access to in real life. I've always attributed this to being a consequence of personal wounds I've amassed over the course of my life, but learning that this was a default mode of operation has made me realize the critical importance of bringing up my repressed center.

After a loved one died, I was in a conversation with a friend regarding the joy and hope of heaven. My friend expressed a deep sense of dread about heaven. I was grieved over her dread and found myself burdened that there were probably others like her. And so, in the midst of the global pandemic, I wrote a small group discussion guide on the topic of heaven and invited any and all who wanted to attend. Twelve weeks of studying the King and kingdom to come, in the midst of political unrest during a tumultuous election year, while experiencing a global pandemic, brought great comfort, peace, and hope to the hearts of the few who gathered in our living room. I couldn't have accomplished leading that study without my understanding of the importance of bringing up my repressed center. I was undoubtedly called to *do* something about the fear others were experiencing and I did, resulting in one of the most satisfying achievements of my lifetime.

BRETT—NINE

What's helped me bring up productive doing in my life has been to organize achievable tasks for myself. I've realized it's impossible for me to manage the cleanliness of our whole house. If my wife or one of our three kids has left something on the couch or on the floor, I generally feel frustrated about it, just step over it, and get on with my day. But I have taken charge of the cleanliness of the kitchen. I know where everything goes, I like the solitude of cleaning the dishes and putting away the food, and I get immense satisfaction from a clean kitchen. Over the years, my wife and I have figured out how to share household responsibilities that leave me feeling like I have agency and can be productively helpful, and leave her feeling like she has a partner and is not the only adult in the household.

Bringing Up Thinking

WHITNEY—ONE

The only way I have learned to manage my dominant center of doing is by bringing up my repressed center of thinking, which means learning new beliefs about my productivity. As a One, my worth, confidence, and identity are tied to my doing. When I am not able to be as productive as I want to be and perform to my standards, I often experience shame, guilt, and frustration. So I have had to intentionally challenge my belief systems about doing. This really became apparent when I became a single mother at twenty-eight years old.

Before then, I was the mother-wife-friend who had all the Pinterest boards, planned detailed theme parties, volunteered to help, and kept every single commitment. I believed that in order to be a good mother-wife-friend, I had to be perfect at doing. And then all of a sudden, I found myself without a partner, with no way to keep the perfect image and to do all the things I had done before. I had to use all of my energy every day just to keep myself afloat and my son happy and healthy.

So I decided that something needed to change. And I started by saying no to things. No to hanging out with friends. No to making fresh nutritious meals every night. No to going the extra mile at work. No to volunteering at the party for my son's class. To help manage this decrease in doing, I started working on my beliefs about my doing. I started engaging in a lot of self-talk. At first, it felt unnatural. And I didn't totally believe the things I was saying to myself, such as: "It's okay to just be getting by some days," and "You are still a good mom if you don't buy those cookies for the party," and "You are allowed to take care of yourself tonight instead of doing the laundry."

My inner critic had a field day during this time. It is a very uncomfortable process to tease apart your worth from your productivity. But by repeating the mantras to myself more and more, my thinking about doing started to shift. My doing became more manageable. And the voice started to quiet down.

HOLLY—TWO

In my work as a minister, I particularly like being the person that my coworkers come to when they are making decisions. I love hearing anything they have to share, talking through issues they have, and dreaming about what "someday" might look like. It's a good week when several people stop by my office for these conversations. Whether I should feel this way or not, the fact that I am needed is extremely life-giving for me.

I just got back from three months of maternity leave. It was so good for me to be away, but I was eager to return to work and my coworkers. Still, immediately after my return I felt unsettled. I especially felt this way when we were all together for staff meetings or when closed-door conversations happened, and I was on the other side of the door. I started acting in unhealthy ways, like pathetically lingering in common spaces waiting for someone to catch up with me. Weeks went by and I was really feeling hurt by the fact that things were not the way they used to be. I felt like I must have done or said something that was terribly wrong. I felt like I had been replaced and I felt sure that I was no longer needed.

At a particularly low moment when I was deep in my feelings and failing when I tried to do something different, it hit me. Even though I've worked with a therapist and a spiritual director for a number of years in an effort to bring up my thinking center, it sometimes takes weeks for me to notice that I'm not using thinking at all. And if I can't add thinking to my pattern of feeling and doing, it never occurs to me that what other people are doing may not have anything to do with me. When I use all three centers, I don't allow my feelings to create false narratives about whether people love me, or want me, or don't.

JILL—SIX

As I do recovery and trauma work, there's one thing I am learning about myself in relationships: once I have allowed someone into my circle of trust, it is profoundly disorienting to learn they might not have the same level of loyalty to me that I do to them. Loyalty has sometimes become uncritical loyalty, which has never served me well. When I have experienced betrayal by people I trusted, it has thrown me into deep shame and fear and caused me to distrust myself and my own experience of reality. As a Six, these experiences have shaken me to my core.

But when I bring up my productive thinking, I'm realizing I don't have to shut down to protect myself when I've been hurt, and I don't have to blame myself for not predicting everything. I can accept these experiences for what they are and experience the empowering feeling that with God's help I have what it takes to move forward and take care of myself. I am learning to lean into my gift of faith and trust that I can face whatever the future brings.

REFLECT AND DISCUSS

1. As you read the story from your number, what stood out to you?

2. What similarities did you see between the stories in your stance?

3. What differences did you see between the stories in your stance?

4. What was most surprising to you in the stories from other stances?

5. What did you learn about the way other stances make their way through the world?

JOURNEY ON

Look over the "Try This" section for your number in part two of *The Journey Toward Wholeness*. Choose one of the transformative possibilities prompts from that section and commit to it for the week. Consider journaling or having a conversation with a trusted person around one of the questions for your number.

6

TRANSFORMATION

The great challenge in seeking transformation is that we have no control over when transformative opportunities will come our way. So, in seeking wholeness, we need to be aware and willing and open to allowing something new to happen.

THE JOURNEY TOWARD WHOLENESS

READ

The Journey Toward Wholeness part two, "Stances: Naming and Managing Your Repressed Center of Intelligence"

CHECK IN

As we enter our last week together, I want you to know that I'm so glad we've been able to be on this journey together. Before we dive into transformation, take some time to share about your week.

- Which transformative possibility prompt did you choose?
- How did it go?
- What did you discover about yourself?

OVERVIEW

We sometimes use the words *change* and *transformation* interchangeably, but I think there is a significant difference between the two. Change is when you take on something new. Transformation occurs when something old falls away, usually beyond your control.

Change is often short-term but don't lose sight of its value because there is a lot of goodness in change. And yet when it comes to our awareness of, and the accompanying desire for, things like transformation and wholeness, we expect to read a few books, attend a seminar, and listen to a podcast or two so we can check these enlightened achievements off the list and then move on to the next one.

It's risky to embark on an intentional journey toward wholeness. There is inherent risk in making a commitment to a more holistic life. It's exciting but challenging to uncover the parts of you that have been protected by your personality—parts that you might discover you don't need anymore. As an example, I am learning, at age seventy, that I don't need to be liked nearly as much as I used to. And it

> There is inherent risk in making a commitment to a more holistic life.

feels so great. We have all experienced disconnection and fragmentation in our lives, so it's hard to imagine what it will be like to discover new ways of feeling more complete. We experience a greater feeling of completion through the process of making free and honest choices about the parts of ourselves that we want to hold on to, and the parts that we have peace in allowing to simply and gently fall away.

REFLECT AND DISCUSS

1. Can you think of something that you intentionally changed? How long did it last?

2. What has changed you?

3. What is changing you now?

4. What has been transformational in your life?

   a. How did that opportunity present itself to you?

   b. What have you been able to allow to fall away on your journey toward transformation?

c. What did you gain?

d. Was it worth it?

JOURNEY DEEPER

The beginning of any transformative work includes increased self-awareness and honest self-reflection. Unfortunately, when we begin to increase self-awareness and when we try to be more self-reflective, the first things we encounter are the parts of ourselves that we don't like. We're acutely aware of the ways we've tried to change and failed. And for many who begin the journey toward transformation, that is reason enough to turn back.

The key to any transformational work is *allowing*. If you could get rid of the things you don't like about yourself, you would have already done it. As it turns out, it isn't as easy as it sounds. That's because we try to rid ourselves of the parts of ourselves that we don't approve of instead of allowing them to fall away. Admittedly, allowing is much more challenging than believing that we can change our behavior any time we choose. If only it was that simple. Spiritual practices are the way we create enough space in our lives to make room for allowing things to happen in their own time. Change is inevitable, but transformation occurs when personality falls away.

> Spiritual practices are the way we create enough space in our lives to make room for allowing things to happen in their own time.

For those who make it past the challenge of loving ourselves enough for the journey, another hurdle is waiting. Much of what longs to be resolved and healed within our families of origin presents itself early in the journey toward transformation and wholeness. Misunderstandings and struggles are remembered at unexpected times. We are newly aware of our own inadequate responses to the people we come from. And this is one of life's journey's that requires honesty. It won't work to rewrite our history. Instead, we will have to allow it to be as we remember, and then we have to make room for it to come along as part of who we are as we continue the journey toward who we hope to become.

Transformation Is a Challenge for Every Enneagram Number

Ones: Resentment is the result of your frustration and dissatisfaction with the imperfection you see in yourself and in the world. Transformation will require that you allow some of that to fall away.

Twos: If you're going to make space for your own journey—a journey that might lead to some transformation—you will have to let go of giving before and beyond what is requested of you.

Threes: The jumping off point for your journey toward transformation is failure, not success. Keep in mind that it's not helpful when you're trying to be something other than you are. This journey is all about authenticity.

Fours: Envy makes the journey toward transformation somewhat treacherous. Believing that something fundamental is missing in you will always be a roadblock. You need to accept on faith that you are not flawed. And then let life teach you that in reality other people don't have inner qualities that you lack. You just have to clear the way so you can see them in yourself.

Fives: Experiences of transformation will require that you give up some of what you keep in your head for something more holistic. What you have in your head, added to what you quietly carry in your heart and combined with what you're capable of learning from listening to your body, will be your introduction to a more holistic way of living. And that will pave the way for you to begin to experience transformation.

Sixes: Your need to feel secure can prevent new ways of seeing the world. People rarely include feeling secure when they share stories about the experiences that transformed their lives. Try to trust opportunities that have the potential to help you reframe your understanding of yourself and your capacity for successfully encountering the world.

Sevens: One of the gifts of the journey toward wholeness is that we find our way together, in community. The gift it holds for you in particular will be the discovery that you can depend on others for what you need. That in itself will be transformative for you. And you will have plenty to offer in return.

Eights: Lust as understood in Enneagram wisdom is ultimately about self-extension and control and independence. Transformation eliminates the need for all three. It's not something you can go get. It insists on a posture of waiting and then it comes to you. Faith and control cannot peacefully coexist. And there is no such thing as a journey toward wholeness that doesn't rely on faith.

Nines: Your propensity for allowing and letting go are necessary for any journey toward wholeness. You are blessed in that both come naturally to you. But they don't replace the need for assertion and participation, which are challenging for you. When much is given, much is required, so your journey will require that you show up, pay attention, fully participate, and find your place among fellow travelers.

REFLECT AND DISCUSS

1. As you have done transformational work, have you had to deal with parts of yourself that you don't like? What did you think, feel, or do?

2. What hurts from your family of origin might you need to forgive and leave behind?

3. What stands out to you about why transformation might be difficult for your number?

4. What has helped you on this journey?

5. What are you willing to give up for transformation?

JOURNEY ON

As we come to the end of this journey together, there is still plenty of goodness waiting to be discovered. I would encourage you to choose a mantra from the two options listed below for your number and commit to spending some good time with it. Perhaps you could put a note on your bathroom mirror or change the lock screen on your phone. You could add it to your daily meditation practice or prayer time.

1s Two things can be true.
And it was good.

2s I can say no.
What do I need?

3s I can allow feelings.
I am more than what I do.

4s My feelings . . . and yours.
Choose the ordinary.

5s Finding comfort in the world.
Be present to the world.

6s Trusting my experience and myself.
All shall be well.

7s I can choose to be satisfied.
All feelings matter.

8s I can slow down.
Vulnerability is not weakness.

9s Decide more, merge less.
Make a choice—I can change my mind.